CONCERT FAVORITES

Volume 1

Band Arrangements Correlated with Essential Elements Band Method Book 1

ISBN 978-0-634-05212-5

HAL•LEONARD®
7777 W. Bluemound Rd. P.O. Box 13819 Milwaukee, WI 53213

00860132

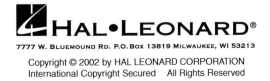

LET'S ROCK!

BARITONE T.C.

MICHAEL SWEENEY (ASCAP)

MAJESTIC MARCH

BARITONE T.C.

By PAUL LAVENDER

MICKEY MOUSE MARCH
(From Walt Disney's "THE MICKEY MOUSE CLUB")

BARITONE T.C.

Words and Music by JIMMIE DODD
Arranged by MICHAEL SWEENEY

00860132

POWER ROCK

(We Will Rock You • Another One Bites The Dust)

BARITONE T.C.

Arranged by MICHAEL SWEENEY

00860132

WHEN THE SAINTS GO MARCHING IN

BARITONE T.C.

Words by KATHERINE E. PURVIS
Music by JAMES M. BLACK
Arranged by JOHN HIGGINS

00860132

FARANDOLE
(From "L'Arlésienne")

BARITONE T.C.

GEORGES BIZET
Arranged by MICHAEL SWEENEY (ASCAP)

00860132

JUS' PLAIN BLUES

BARITONE T.C.

MICHAEL SWEENEY (ASCAP)

00860132

From the Paramount and Twentieth Century Fox Motion Picture TITANIC

MY HEART WILL GO ON

(Love Theme From 'Titanic')

Music by JAMES HORNER
Lyric by WILL JENNINGS
Arranged by PAUL LAVENDER

BARITONE T.C.

00860132

From THE MUPPET MOVIE

THE RAINBOW CONNECTION

Words and Music by PAUL WILLIAMS
and KENNITH L. ASCHER
Arranged by PAUL LAVENDER

BARITONE T.C.

From Walt Disney's MARY POPPINS

SUPERCALIFRAGILISTICEXPIALIDOCIOUS

Words and Music by
RICHARD M. SHERMAN and ROBERT B. SHERMAN
Arranged by MICHAEL SWEENEY

BARITONE T.C.

(From "THE SOUND OF MUSIC")

DO-RE-MI

BARITONE T.C.

Lyrics by OSCAR HAMMERSTEIN II
Music by RICHARD RODGERS
Arranged by PAUL LAVENDER

00860132

…UMS OF C…NA

BARITONE T.C.

MICHAEL SWEENEY (ASCAP)

LAREDO
(Concert March)

BARITONE T.C.

JOHN HIGGINS

POMP AND CIRCUMSTANCE
March No. 1

BARITONE T.C.

By EDWARD ELGAR
Arranged by MICHAEL SWEENEY

STRATFORD MARCH

BARITONE T.C.

JOHN HIGGINS (ASCAP)